ANVIL ON A SHOESTRING

MIKE SILVERTON

Some of the writings collected here were first published, often in a different form, in the 1960s and '70s in *Harper's*, *The Nation*, *Wormwood Review*, *Poetry Now*, *some/thing*, *Chelsea*, *Prairie Schooner*, *Elephant*, and other publications. Several appeared in anthologies published by William Cole: *Eight Lines and Under* (Macmillan, 1967), *Pith and Vinegar* (Simon and Schuster, 1969), *Poetry Brief* (Macmillan, 1971), and *Poems One Line & Longer* (Grossman, 1973).

An alternate version of *Light Summer Reading* is read by the author on *Analogue Smoque*, a two-CD set (Pogus 21029-2) with musical accompaniments by Tom Hamilton and Al Margolis.

Duodenal Etiquette: Scènes de Ballet and *The Dada Within* were published in 2021 in *Exacting Clam*.

© 2022 by Mike Silverton

All Rights Reserved.

Set in Janson Text with LATEX.

ISBN: 978-1-952386-31-2 (paperback)
Library of Congress Control Number: 2021949129

Sagging Meniscus Press
Montclair, New Jersey
saggingmeniscus.com

In Loving Memory
Lemmó Djūste,
Minnesota's State Aphorist, 1887–1919

*The bat lives in a world
painted in shades of its own voice.*

—Gordon Grice, "Bat Country"

Contents

General-Purpose Poems   *1*

Light Summer Reading   *71*

Paths to the Caliph's Boudoir: With Magic-Lantern Slides   *81*

The Enchanted Kielbasa: An die ferne Geliebte   *97*

Duodenal Etiquette: Scènes de Ballet   *147*

The Dada Within   *155*

ANVIL ON A SHOESTRING

General-Purpose Poems

If I hit myself on the head with a rock
will I confuse my phrenologist?

I extract a being from the miasma,
the kind that spits in the holes it makes in its benefactors.
I toss it back. The miasma lifts. The miasma returns.

GENERAL-PURPOSE POEMS

Monsieur Pierre:
dents frame the face,
a "bulbous reticule" (Vesalius).
M'lle Marie:
painful to look at.
M'sieur Pierre & M'lle Marie ensemble:
cheeks, blotched; eyes, crusted; thoughts, acidic.
Incoherencies well from "impris'ning lips (kiss! kiss!)
& gums & toofs" (Piranesi).
Truant smirks encircle cigars, in her case, Pierre's,
in his case, Marie's, & vice versa,
lower lips shov'ling faces unlovingly, swelling untemptingly,
tittering, puckering, rejuvenating nothing,
maneuvering nowhere, moreover poorly,
four feet treading air.
And so, to you both, blemishes withal,
instructions:
ingest these modification lozenges,
sit back and wait.

Fugitive grapes empurple one's face
                            or, better, shouldn't.
  In the distance, off hilly hummocks, hummocky hillocks,
tumpy knolls, spiney ridges, peaky pikes, soaring highlands, craggy
summits, towering ridges, rolling knaps, hog's-back chines, downy
                                  barrows, & loamy
                                           steppes
   bounce raindrops clothed as fugitive grapes (see above),
      as here, I fear, a brackish, backwater vintage
                                  besots.

GENERAL-PURPOSE POEMS

A burgher being nipped at by moths hits upon a stratagem.
"Moths, you devour a kinsman," he cries
and scarfs a woolen to prove it
and dies.

ANVIL ON A SHOESTRING

The suave stranger is, among provincials, pelvis deep in gallantries.
Suave stranger: "Such children! Such homes!"
The rubes: "And on this rock we chisel our thanks."
Suave stranger: "Rotary! Elks! Masonic temples!"
The bumpkins: "You're getting better, but start running anyhow.
Jump aboard Sis. Thank her and keep running on this peg-leg
we do wish you'd let us install
just as soon as we're finished sawing off your real one
so that, crossing the nation, you'll leave a dotted line
we thought might look nice to the eye for details,
like the little perforations in tear-here packaging."
Suave stranger: "Hoorah for the Bedouin under the mulch
& indomitable peoples everywhere!"
The hayseeds: "The eyelid never flies but trembles
beneath the brow like a fat curtain.
Your head & your liver. Your change.
A pleasure!"

GENERAL-PURPOSE POEMS

Devolution the grimace extracts. Where it was is now a hole.

"I stand here. With you."
"Yes."
"Comrade, they ascend!"
"Yes."
Both men linger on one foot apiece,
flamingoly.
A committee removes the promontory on which
the comrades stand, initiating land reforms.

GENERAL-PURPOSE POEMS

Night yields to morn & out stagger the walking wounded,
my recalcitrant feet, hauling yours instanter, the dilutest echo
of Tu Fu and Erroll Flynn, O poignant hybrid, haranguing the mists
yet again.
Ne'rtheless,
it gives one pleasure to have taken part in Art.
You look better & I found something else to write:

> The busy wind shed drops on my bed & on my pillow,
> from where did I rise, so rare a blossom was,
> musick heard I! And skylarks skylarking! And O! the syllables!

But I am too young to die!
So let's call it irony.
Good enough, says he, climbing into a barrel,
barreling down the thoroughfare,
earning interest here & there,
this whimsical rascal! Pass the Cheez Whiz. Casimir
is on his knees, farming. Piled high with old smelts, Casimir's lady
                    refuses to be gai. Elsewhere,
I enrolled in a course called Paths to the Caliph's Boudoir. For the
      first hour
our instructor showed us how, with a mere fingernail,
the Successor to the Believers scratched one concubine's portrait
on another concubine's bosom
and got away with it.

GENERAL-PURPOSE POEMS

May I borrow your paisley ascot?
I want to garrote myself with a view to being remembered
as fashion's tragicmost figure.

The old khan drowns in secretions & we, hélas,
wax ungoverned. A citrus rind descends,
suggesting succession
if not exactly orthodoxy.

What this appears to be is a paean to transition
which I conduct with a railroad tie,
& how great a success it is,
for you have arisen & slidden away,
& I am strong and handsomer.

A sunny spot,
the entrance to a cloister. Fountain,
grassy banks, trees. The ladies
sing of the garden's pleasures, sunshine,
flowers.
    The King of the Moors creeps in
& whispers of love. Elisabetta flutters, a page announces Rodrigo,
Mercury intervenes, a monk exits,
a sailor steps forward & explains knots.

Aboriginals, we learn, irradiate each other with sign language.
Explosions mark the hours (none louder than an angry thought, but it's the thought that counts).
A leak in the daylight is best seen at night.

GENERAL-PURPOSE POEMS

Seriously, it makes no difference.
Even so, tell me where you live and I'll tell you
what you should be doing.
Why requires different information,
but would that be interesting?
Mother relished carrots, couldn't get enough.
She burst. I tried to stanch the flow.
Does it matter? To you, I mean.
One tick, one tock,
a sliver of time, inagile at best,
but does anyone notice or care?
Inagile rhymes with Tintagel, but really,
does anyone even know who Arnold Bax is?

ANVIL ON A SHOESTRING

A hand dangles & sizzles amongst fennel-scented cutlets.
Light lies lightly on the lit.
The merlot uncorks (ploop!) autokinetically.
The deck called poop fizzles out entirely
as the Hesperus sinks.
I hear you clinging to a wintergreen Lifesaver out there
in the goop & strange to tell,
it isn't so much your yawp's randomness
as the lace upon windswept waves,
some bits of which spell *water*.

GENERAL-PURPOSE POEMS

The fork in the road has two tines. A malevolent layabout
plunges a spatula into a passerby at an otherwise gracious time of day
with its tawny, Bordelaise sunbeams.

You go to the window to see what the weather's like,
come away with a high paying job
excellent benefits
perks.

Amazing.
Innumerable people think briefly and concur.
Amazing.

GENERAL-PURPOSE POEMS

Have you ever seen a silver dollar upside down?
It sticks out its little feet!
It turns itself right over again!

What fools, my friend. One picks up another
& the gunk, akimbo, oozing downtown
swallows the acrobatics. This is the low point.

GENERAL-PURPOSE POEMS

One succumbs to caprice and leaps, for instance,
specific distances.

People bounce. (But not always.)
Hope remains the tutor, even in despair.
Are the gods all dead?

Non! Pas de tout!
They lie on their abdomens, munching god food.

If you say so. What's the time?

Two-thirty.

A man with the incorrect head holds mitigation to lie in a hairpiece. Insight is elusive.

GENERAL-PURPOSE POEMS

The food drops off a fork,
slithers through a gut,
out an anus,
shit. Tish

enters from the garden.
"100,000 pardoons, Rolf,
I thought you was alone!"

Excellency:
Allow me to clarify my position.
I am getting out of the dragoon business.
I am wholly absorbed with walking away from the dragoon business.
Boom tiddy boom.

GENERAL-PURPOSE POEMS

The corpse on the pavement? Funny you should ask.
The P of WASSERMAN PHARMACY's dismantling sign,
the shop he intended to patronize, brained him.
He required a bedpan. Wasserman. Get it? Irony.

L'Éminence Grise turns out to be nothing more bodeful
than a mammalian tangible rotting in such good taste
as one had thought improbable. You mistake my mood.
I am not sad. My joie stepped out to be cast in bronze.

GENERAL-PURPOSE POEMS

Ahead, in the confusion, the tongue.
When you think, it pokes you in the eye. When you ail,
it flounders on the carpet, a tacky flap demanding attention.
You restrain it with your foot at your comfort's expense.

The triumph Destiny marked me for missed & landed
on a fermented black bean now doing business
second only to La Choy.

GENERAL-PURPOSE POEMS

If we should happen to meet post mortem, adjust my features to
    benignity
and set me astride a porpoise instructed in the way to a pleasing void.

ANVIL ON A SHOESTRING

I climbed over the wreckage to purchase men's hose,
                size ninety-five.

Size ninety-five, please.

Can ninety-five possibly be your size, sir?

Obviously not.
I am planning to use them as overnight bags
as my luggage was destroyed in the recent catastrophe.

We haven't any size ninety-five. How about some nice anesthesia?

Thanks, no. But I will take a rabbit's foot.

What size, sir?

Small please.
I am shy among animals.

GENERAL-PURPOSE POEMS

Another summer night leaping off edges,
in thrall to false imperatives.
Indoors! To bed! that I might again dream
of the goddess who waters the parched.

Birds take wing, ah, effortlessly
even with feathers stuck in their asses
& here toil I, rooting for diction,
with my tongue in my one good ear.

A glimmer I espy in a copse far off but
ill equipt am I to pursue, as
I wear one shoe
only.
                This shoe,
it knows what it knows!

ANVIL ON A SHOESTRING

Take for example an armful of creweled wastebaskets.
Take as another an armful of cruel, wasteful swamp gaboons.
Compare them, baskets to gaboons. Imagine one of the latter,
Muthaless, hamstringing people he lulls to complaisance
by batting his long lashes, devouring them whole & spitting out the
      buttons.
Imagine now that Muthaless disappears in the plumbing with
explosives. And so, as you pick lath, plaster,
& Muthaless morceaux
from your person, you e
vaporate.

Bonded to these duck-waddle feet,
the head goes abobbing down the street,
the envy of the stuck-in-place.

The loaves one had cast upon the waters return
for cereal numbers. The yak loafs in its wilderness quarters,
informing the air with yakkish malaise.
A sky hook transports the poet to where business parks aren't.

On the southern continent surefoot boys
of the woolly llama request, And now please delight us,
or so it is taken by the idiom-indigent traveler
plying to the littoral.
Arrived none the wiser, he gestures to purchase a knit bonnet
& leaves, misunderstood,
with a stone idol abrading his scalp,
from the Lake Titicaca region.
Traveler struggles up dusty cobbles.
Shopkeepers gawk.
Perspective swallows.
Flags of the nations of América del Sur,
lofty yet consternating symbols of hope,
go cheese yourselfs! (Queso!)

The detached retinue aches to embrace a footloose
ophthalmologist. Pitching camp in his absence,
they exercise the jaws on pemmican. For amusement,
the Poetry Committee composes a conceit about farts
people with taste urge them to abandon:

> Wind passes over the lake.
> The swelling waves stretch away
> without limit. Autumn returns with twilight,
> & boats grow rare on the river.

GENERAL-PURPOSE POEMS

The necktie, you ask.
A tapeworm misapplied, a pet,
a friend, and so on.
No sooner spake than thunder thundered,
lightning lit, and so on.
Finality draws nigh for you and I (me),
plus that other matter.

ANVIL ON A SHOESTRING

Reader, your time is better spent at topiary.
I have in mind a large horse, of box perhaps,
stuffed with gooseberry Greeks positioned at a long, tall wall of
    viburnum
or holly. Or, perhaps, forsythia. Begin soon
lest the rim greaper take thee where the sun don't shine
on botanical gardens.

GENERAL-PURPOSE POEMS

Did you shit yourself, Bacchus? Forgive me,
it's the bacchanal I smell a day late.

Panicking hordes can be interesting.
Many attractive paintings of panicking hordes.
A crumhorn's baleful *honk* obtains.

GENERAL-PURPOSE POEMS

Survivalist Advisory:
Nail dwelling to planet,
bedroom door shut,
robe to door,
slippers to floor,
tongue to chin.
Hope for the best.

So that, friends, when it looks (I mean really, truly looks)
as if I bought the plantation, put a long summer squash in the coffin,
or if you can afford it, a marzipan effigy,
sit me upright on something heading elsewhere
and rejoice! Nibble figs and go plink on your lutes.

GENERAL-PURPOSE POEMS

"Teleology is the moralizing of chronology."
Arriving on a sunbeam, an enigma encounters a bottleneck.

ANVIL ON A SHOESTRING

It unsettles you, this gnashing and frothing?
Have you thought about departing?
If, however, you prefer to remain,
your foot, yes, the blue one, is best installed
between Alphonse and Gaston.

GENERAL-PURPOSE POEMS

My prince, I bring a disquietude.
The townspeople are behaving oddly at and about the well.
This excites the prince's curiosity.
Upon arriving at the well,
the prince and first minister discover the townspeople chanting in
    pidgin,
exchanging directions in Old Church Slavonic
and dancing La Lala, ineptly, la.
Do you suppose, asks the prince, that this behavior has something to
    do with the well?
Putting the question to a test, the prince and first minister sip the
    well water.

Quite suddenly, all about returns to normal.

Triangulation's the hot ticket here.
Lute-plucking trouvères fall into the pit de
spondency dug. Witty, agile, fetching, keen,
none of this counts under stacked trouvères.

Remember the bee our breakfast bewitched,
shore birds cavorting? My solo ukulele?
Remember when we'd no further need to stand on edge
in kiosks? "Welcome, please, park where you like,
except perhaps on the Great Spirit's foot."
It heartened me, your mind's veiled gong, closer perhaps
to an offstage trombone, out there on the terrace,
in answer to my alphorn's *blap!*

One swam to a music a bit like *La Mer*,
where giant squid were loath to appear.
The sun was setting, one was likely to drown,
swimming home from France.
Had one been wanton, too over the top?
Should one have combed the Transbaykal Steppe
for a music bluer-collar in tone?

One thinks of the score,
of household hints,
of attractively priced yet ominous yams,
of nostril exams.

GENERAL-PURPOSE POEMS

Say you intend to collect oysters. Start at the pearl
and work toward an edge. Setting aside the viscous dumpling,
paint a Templar's cross on the shell and name it Freida. Teach it to
    fetch.
Pause to reflect what a prairie might look like
rolled up and stuffed in a drain.

We understand, first, that certain attractions are glandular.
One thinks of a rutting Doppelgänger, blushes
and turns the page, a prudent gesture
leading anywhere.

Halve Maen at anchor. Ship's Master Hudson,
jawbone for exploration set, nibbles lodestone.
Tableaux slip away. Or is this merely
impaired vision contorting in a manner
unbecoming to historical nautica?
A peruke ripples at an open window
(a term by sailors frowned upon).

She remembers bananas. You giggle.
She impugns your tact but let's let that slide.
Her thoughts about bananas dwell in the abstract,
neither of the stunted, apple-flavored kind
nor the kind one cooks with, and one wonders why.
Bananas in the elsewhere,
as invisible as the Iron Chancellor's silk underwear.
She thinks about bananas
even here on Coco Chanel's Maginot Line.

To fire off ripostes like separating Velcro,
to brandish glandular commas at table,
to sniff one's fingers and guess which hand,
to lean against momentum without capsizing,
to dream of the tabernacle pump out there in the evangelical night,
chuf, chuf, chuf! Christ on a cracker!
It is as the game warden cautions: Fishing twice as fast is still fishing.

ANVIL ON A SHOESTRING

There in the cloakroom, Respighi, dead.
Something to fear? Or, better, ponder?
A comet approaches.
Something else to worry about.
If you and your glissandi float away like a violist's dozen (11)
even early in the morning, it's no accident,
especially here, as the Hesperus bobs at anchor.

I'd love for you to gape all agog, the lobster's look en route to the pot.
Perhaps on the way we might have a word,
send you to school, hope
for the best.

Before my lips could, a commissar's did.
Lumpens dream of Leninist females, dialectically naked
and ripe. In the victory exercise,
Stakhanovites prosper, accompanied by running dogs
nipping at the heels of off-White Guards.
And Trotsky steps out for a refill (he says).
It is clear in art that we must consider where to look.
Paper lanterns bathe a five-year feast in a flattering light,
yet have we the desire, the proletarian grit
to illumine the motherland's warts?
A tongue out for viewing is a tongue out for viewing
(here certainly, there perhaps),
monarchical throats bared for the slitting,
and on the phonograph, snap, crackle, pop.
Respighi in bewilderment blinks.

GENERAL-PURPOSE POEMS

I notified the chasm inspector about a chasm I happened upon
on my way home from my place of employment. He was so pleased
he rewarded me with a box of yodel spume
and a ride on the sunset machine.

A person of my acquaintance asked me one evening,
What is poetry?
Poetry, I replied, is like a pump.
Look, I said,
imagine you've been tossed off a roof by hoodlums.
Where would you find solace?
In poetry!
You would do well to read poetry all the time.
To signal the close of my talk I drew and flourished a little silver
    scimitar
I carry for such moments.

You may ask, Do you have a moped?
I do. On it father hones the carving knife and it has worn away.
Father carves and I serve, thinking of this recentmost honing
and a withered moped standing forlornly in metal shavings.
Father goes to the tavern and boasts about how sharp he keeps the
      knife.
I don't think he hears me sobbing at night as he fumbles upstairs.
It's no bigger now than a briefcase.

ANVIL ON A SHOESTRING

When you jumped aboard the wagonette heading to the Cowgirl
    Ball,
a mother pinched a moose and spoke in measured syllables:
I recognize you by your farmer-cheese diction.
I recognize you by your rainbow polyps.
Guessing her mind, you offered a scoop of azure edibles et un Avion
    Surpris.
A daisy striking roadside poses got a coat of dust for its trouble.
You had no time for nature, you were off to the Cowgirl Ball!
The opening ceremony featured me firing a raft cannon to provide
    the merrymakers
with a chance to guess the speed at which I depart lakes backwards.

When I see my love at the rendezvous I have an uneasy feeling.
My love looks like a Claymore mine. Ah, but wait! And, and yet!
My love is gorgeous where she works! where tubes are tested free of
    charge
At Kantor the Kabinet King's. I bring my tubes for her to test.

If an odor persists, it might be thought.
Think. Give it a try. We'll call you a tiger
and avoid stepping on you.

The first summer fog closing over the Prebilovs
saw people fumbling through the streets to rejoice with their friends.
The fog is here! they shouted.
Good luck to you, Ivan said to the fog.
Ivan was pounding Ellen. Peering through the fog,
He looked her over. She resembled somebody's baggy pants.
Ivan began pounding harder.
Her bobbing head gazed up at him.
My eyes are swimming and my brain is all awhirl, Ellen said to Ivan.
Is my back swelling?
Looks puffy, answered Ivan.
Then you ought to stop soon, Ellen suggested.

One crystal-dazzling afternoon (viz., Swarovsky)
I fed a pigeon Sienna-brown peanuts (viz., UPS delivery trucks).
It perched on my ankle, it ate from my hand,
it scratched the calf of my right crossed leg,
creating white lines of unsettled epithelium.

Sunrise! You annihilate the night!
But I am not stupid all the time, someone visit me, please.
I will sneeze. You see,
I always thought it was cunning to be an odious baby.
But I am not for you, my friend. I am dead.
You are dead?
Yes, I am dead. Don't be sad,
I'll make you a field marshal and give you this low horse to ride on.
It's just like riding a bicycle.

This poem sets out to describe the inadequacy of general anesthesia.
The world needs something stronger.
As the President of the United States has so often asked,
Why do we jump up and down on our grandfathers?
Better to dream of Galileo, awaken and weep.

Fate's fickle finger flicks flowers off lapels. Prenez garde!
Fate anticipates developments.
You stick out your tongue. Fate says put it back.

Light Summer Reading

NTERHUNDS have a multilateral appeal. Falling off a roof, one looks about for an Unterhund. Anyway, there one goes. A cat on a windowsill observes the late-afternoon sun reflecting in one's eyes. A passerby follows one's descent with his Rolleiflex, fussing with the focus knob. He anticipates a collision.

Now one cannot spare anything, least of all the time. So those were the days.

On account of the felons sprawled about the house, mother thinks of herself as a failure. One gathers them up, taking care not to bruise their tender tips, and stacks them in a corner.

Not long ago one discovered mother rummaging a hundred or so yards ahead of herself. In view of the situation's metaphysical complexion, one wonders: What defines her search? One of her possible ladies-in-waiting—that's the future for you, bristling with erotic possibilities—provides me with clothing in styles as yet unimagined. Consequently, one has the wardrobe for a life a good deal more speculative than the life one leads.

One sometimes speaks to women one first observes through one's periscope. In general, one behaves glandularly. Owing to the periscope's narrow field of vision, one loses sight of the big picture. One fails to note in the mountain range out there on the horizon, the inflatable kind one orders from catalogs, a pouch in a valley ideal for rearing progeny.

When one's feet stipple the landscape, one cannot tell where one is. One is too proud to ask people walking who knows where, 'Can you point me in a direction?'

Now as one stipples, hither and thither, the least engaging of mother's ladies-in-waiting introduces one to a tribe of Native Americans one assumed was extinct, the Ugh-Excised Unterhunds. One refrains from saying 'How!' yet one is uncertain that one is behaving like the sophisticate one longs to become.

The man wearing the incorrect head degrades his reputation among thoughtful people by presuming the remedy to lie in a toupee. The key to transparency is even more elusive than a teeny weeny bug in a big leafy tree.

They are humorless on the floor, these teeny weeny, sleep-deprived bugs, down there on the carpet in the middle of the night, where, to be fair, they're no more trouble than seated in teeny weeny highchairs at two in the afternoon, awaiting developments.

One recalls starving when father neglected to pay the bills. Mother would knock him to the floor, run up and down the length of him and slam the trapdoor on his head till his neglectfulness subsided.

It's actually Helmut who explains this in the parlor where starched guests are watching father sitting astride his hand-painted decoy.

One adjusts the vista. The aspects are just there, like another language. One could call it parsing the view. Just parsing through. Parsersby and lily pads.

You may have noticed one's neck. One tells people one's membrum virile also takes a size 17 collar. One has little else to make oneself intriguing. One sits behind a waterfall looking ectoplasmic.

The important thing is, one comes first. One is the first person singular, even here at the bottom of Column A, where one really doesn't care what anybody thinks.

'Yes!' exclaims an Unterhund. 'These utterances embroider a theme I find to my taste.' Clearly, this is a sophisticated Unterhund. We favor sophisticated Unterhunds, even with their dilemmas stitched up in their carcasses like that last grand flourish of a surgical procedure, even with their problems caroming about their crania, careering, ricocheting, exiting multiply.

In the patois of the diocese where Unterhunds worship, one whups an Unterhund's head upside. While one's not sure that's quite the way one puts it, one really has no desire for patois fluency. One does not much fuss over Unterhund expressiveness, tho one is certain that prayer and informal English offer certain rewards. Here, for example, one might observe entirely reasonably, pointing at the sky, is an ambiguous enterprise zone. 'If ever I said such, my flock would depart in a huff,' a shepherd observes. He used to be a shy boy, this shepherd, an Unterhund with a shepherd's crook and syrinx, and the kind of outer garment one sees in certain Christmas cards. He used to ride past one's house in a sack. 'I am riding by wildly,' one would hear him shout but never really knew where the good news was coming from.

That's all over now. It would be imprudent to remove the ceiling to see what comes next. For example, dropping 1000 billion aspirin from the air. They thought it was snow, the first they'd ever seen. They started spreading salt before they caught on. So that makes 1000 billion lightly salted aspirin strewn about a distant place.

Tolstoy said, 'Spray the gentry with sweat and manure, sprinkle the serfs with rosewater. Then let's talk about attitude.'

One's bric-a-brac includes a dollhouse filled with rare novelties. One levitates briefly and falls back to earth, the rare novelties of one's dollhouse strewn about like homunculi.

A crowd gathers and watches dad watching a stand-in sitting astride the hand-painted decoy. Chinese mists arise from the gorge. Someone in the crowd initiates a community sing, beginning with 'O How I Cherish Arranging Flowers from My Window with My Old Canoe Paddle, Hey Ho,' moving right along to the old marching song, 'Owing to Our Fatherland's Clement Climate, the Flowers Achieve a Standard of Deportment to Which All Aspire!'

One sticks one's finger in a grommet.

All that remains is the long reverberation of one's having performed 'The Iconoclast Vanishes' in a palatially vacant space. Let me try to clear that up. The iconoclast vanished but not necessarily where one takes a number and waits. In the way of small pleasures, one remarks one's song's lengthy fade in the space in which the iconoclast comprises an insubstantial presence or absence.

One stands, arms out, palms upward, anticipating expectations. One is, after all, a futurist. We futurists have the properties of seeds.

In your personalized hillbilly hat with corncob pipe and turkey feather, you will fit right in to lawn parties attended by people who look to you as a fresh source of merriment. Don't sulk, we were all stupid once. Nothing to be ashamed of. Wear your personalized hillbilly hat with an easy conscience, eat barbecued ribs and walk around in a spiral which will take you to a boomtown where the music of celebration will go through you like a dose of salts.

Then we shall embrace a daintier you and say, 'How young, how charming,' as the decorative boomtown herons drop like flies.

And only now the golden Unterhunds, their bellies awash in brazen moles, tear themselves from the bosoms of their families. Weeks on end you'd hear them bellowing like regretful incompetents.

How once so young, how once so charming, the herons keep dropping, and now so old, peach-pit scrotums. This, despite everything, is an authentic imagining in which an Unterhund is made to look enigmatic. There is no apparent sense of strain, neither is there cost.

Come along, we are in the way. The incense rises in a thick lilac haze. We gaze at our ensembles in the lagoon's mirror calm, one in one's tails and bullet-proof dickey, you in your chic, shoulder-launched sheath.

In the great scheme of things, one is less than a duster's feather snagged on a hinge of a Chinese screen covered with impressions of mist-enshrouded mountains. The trick in these old Chinese screens is to locate the scholar. Sometimes they're so well integrated into the scenery, these scholars, you never find them. One is reminded of the sound a wind-turbine makes when it rolls off a flatbed.

When Aleuts were new to their island chain, a herpetologist lay in ambush. No Aleut could withstand him! He slew them to crimson mists with sweeping disciplinary glances. Aleuts fled when they saw the brute charging or indeed when they thought he might have mayhem in mind. During a fragile truce, the herpetologist reveals an elaborately decorated breastplate. On one quadrant, forged to resemble a giant amusement shovel, we see a repoussé hand pointing to a repoussé sea.

The Übermensch's belovèd arrives. He tosses her coat in the crapper. For the Übermensch, conventions are instantaneous, to hell with precedents. If one has to ask, one is insufficiently steeped in Übermenschkeit. Everything else goes to charity. And you, tardy Unterhund, you missed the boat, so you while away your days with that peculiar dockside look, as though somewhere about your person a clue to the question, Is there Life after Departure? Worth living, that is. And behind you, the old cottage. And behind the old cottage, you again, Unterhund, sighing with the aspens.

Emotion in opera is paramount. We are interested not so much in what our hero, heroine or villain may do as in how he or she feels before, during and after the action. When Mabooboo learns that Prulala has been captured—remember, he supposes her to be his mother—his thoughts turn to incest, but rather than dashing off as one would in life, he steps stage front and sings of his mad desire.

The aria, 'Tell me of my placenta,' shows as plain as music may that Mabooboo's affection is genuine and that she in turn, the mystery guest, has given him her heart, exclusive of aorta.

Gypsy smugglers descend, dragging female acquisitions. Then follows the first of the beautiful quartets for which this act is famous, 'This is your shithole now.'

For opera's larger requirements, gold dust adorns the very fog! This is, in opera, how one falls in love.

The noise one's parents made dropping dead on the piano when one told them one's adopted, that's music too.

Like the rocks you imagine in bird-like flight, enthusiasts come and go. From the orchestra pit rises the tragic motive of vengeance, jealousy and death, booming forth in terrible significance.

An extraneous sound echoes through the dark forest. The wee woodland creatures attend.

We see these things more clearly on paper. After the pseudonymous Pierre bloodies the nose of his identical twin, the authentic Pierre, he stomps melons plump with seed. Thus from snits do harvests arrive.

We slink about the landscape, clinging to the margins like periwinkles. It is difficult to ignore the creamy spots.

They are young, etc., they eat off placemats. They floss.

One discovers the bridegroom among the spasms.

You recall tastes, sensations, focus knobs and urges. Now it's not the same.

Paths to the Caliph's Boudoir

With Magic-Lantern Slides

Imagine (a challenge!)

Patent-leather shoes, dove-grey spats, shiny silk top hat,
black opal stickpin, embroidered waistcoat,
accessorized cane, golden dental highlights,
in a word, oneself, the poet,
at your disposal and for your reading pleasure.
Further (too soon?), inapposite whispers,
like flatulence in togas (slide, please).
Poetry distributes upon stygian waters paroxysmal imagery, hoop la!
also to the indifferent skies (slide, please), ah,
how calm! And here at an epic's helm we salute the treetops,
line-drying bed linens, their erotica aflutter for all to see
(and snicker at).
An unfortunate turn, you say? So are mudslides.
Poetry is often hard.

A smudge of ether in mufti encircles a maiden,
she of the hinged ear, as another seeks domesticity,

another to host a gala, and here comes yet another
on some still more meddlesome errand
with its long, languid side effects.
This melancholia, it's global. We haul it around like a national debt,
like a liver pickled in Plumber's Helper, and look for applause,
which I once spelled applesauce, can you believe it?
Pin tails to donkeys (slide, please)?
Perpetuity to perps? Apices to zits? And who can say why
or that matters will improve? The poet discovers
a shopworn manatee smiling up from an ostensible sincerity,
yesterday's crises, nursed grudges, cloudy businesses,
inedible smudges, a weakness for squandering what little vitality
mostly at night as starlight identifies luggage tags.

At the top of one's form one engages target-hearts.
Here at the harmonium, Polyhymnia,
one discovers enchanting chords arising
from a formerly dormant apparatus.
It wants a fine-tuned purpose to mark a disconsolate flea.
Operatic storms, as far away as cryptic achievements
burst upon the scene awash in longings
in under-inflated water wings, in thoughts afloat in old brain juice.
Yet via poetry one is saved, ennobled even, set aflame!
It's monumental, this moment! And
no less so the course of events tossing the poet from pillar to pedestal,
a comrade in one's own arms!
One wipes away a droplet of some distant storm or anecdote,
its salient feature men in nightshirts filling temples
with munched-upon lemur tendons.

Smoke is one thing, banana sparks another (slide, please).
Battery-powered moonlight for ersatz events is commensurate and apt.
The sky one inhales, the vague mountaintops, the true-blue motherland,
I! yes, I! welcome the intercontinental stranger, Masoud,
peeling off a ceiling, speaking something.
He is building a flotation device, pontoons en poitrine,
his aero-bosom beginning as a hundred harmonious stumps,
many with their own little feet and itty-bitty attitudes.
Masoun womanizes 24/7 (slide, please).
Sportswriters cheer encouragement, but Masoun,
he isn't happy. There was a lady for doleful example who expired
of perforations from one of Masoun's overtures (slide, please).
No use putting it there any more, such was the consensus.

With your perfect figure and elegant frock, you are one strange sirrah,
sirrah. Why that should be I cannot explain, sirrah replies and dies,
far too interesting to have long survived
this world and its routines.

One dozen vertically aligned insect eyes : : : : : : : : : : : :

The Slope Serenade:
"Upon boughs, birds. Urania sorts undergarments.
We quantify epiphanies as cardinal and ordinal.
Cardinal: Art plucks Voice from Silence's jaws.
Ordinal: The poet, much reduced, contents himself with crumb
    arrangements
distributed randomly across a steppe, O Jesu! Kapok! Whizz! (Slide,
    please.)

And here are cautious pirogi negotiating oil slicks,
hastening toward an armistice,
fangs sheathed in velvet lops (oops, lips).
A primate speaks. Unch. His chin massages his nose (slide, please).
He is unusual. He is a passenger through real and unreal estate,
stagestruck and multidimensional, his last great thought:
Noise first, significance later. And here one teeters on Time's squishy
      cusp,
at a peristaltic surge's inception
with twenty or more sidearms concealed about one's person.
One is nothing but reassuring lumps. En garde!
They infiltrate ashore, draped in debt.
Those two over there, for example, with a shrewd house pet in tow,
a lothario dog with big black mustachios and fantasy reforms (slide,
      please).

Doctor, a foreign body asks, were I to become completely idiomatic
could we then be friends?

What better spot for the Fickle Herd Lied?
"When I looked at what I was doing
I thought I was leaking,
so I repaired to the sultan's turret
where I fell out of bed
and you, colors, you were there,
and Mister Fog asleep in the fogbox."

Adieu, he cried.
How can this be? she warbled in dismay.

Did it seem very long? he asked. Place the victim's nose on your chest
and start rocking. Returning in love,
he walked among embodiments of womankind
and paused, overcome.

The fisherman flies his fish kite at night waiting for a skypike to bite.
The poet applies his hat to his scalp,
bids adieu to commemorative postage, arriving in the countryside
where dusk reveals what millions are indifferent to,
with, for charity, herpetology, left to its own devices.
The poet thinks he sees a thing or two
(a business opportunity and the old homestead).
He thought he heard the trees enquiring (slide, please) up whose xylem?
And here, by stealth, infiltrators whose presence we detect
with devices best left in vague outline.
Enough that gloomy happenstance cements one to listlessness.
However, sometimes it's nice getting pushed around in the dark.
I am pleased withal to have created an instrument of national identity.
You look better and I found something to keep idle hands busy.
Action uncorked goes flat. These rocks can use some torque.
God has and eats his angel cake and pisses spirits intact.

Connections can be just allusive enough to justify a hernia.

Lovers in a bakery:
Adorable dusted with flour, cavorting among the bun racks.
In the plumber's he loves her all over, elbows, nipples, drains, the works.
It is as if a fiery hand clutched him with its fiery iron clutcher (slide,
please). O you dear little fellow, your waist so small,

your bottom so plump and dimpled, and your skin!
You have such a little face I cannot even ooo it.
Your hair so red and fawn-like luxurious, such little hands,
such little feet! Surely nature intended you for a girl
when she gave you this fresh little cock to confuse us with.
Do you like me to tickle it? O yes, dear honey!
I like it very much indeed (slide, please), for I am the lowest swine
and you made me that way. Thinkest you so? Watch this, she said,
and that's not all. Now you're talking! Thinkest you so?
Watch this. And you made me that way.

We pick up the other thread:
Borek A-Cid's mother receives a caller who finds her pinned
To a Biedermeier fainting couch by a Bed Bath Crypt & Beyond
drapery rod. This is likely, the coroner explains,
because the body is quite decomposed
and climate cannot take the blame for everything.
A calling card appended: Legislator Comely / Attachments a Spécialité.
He is known to the demi-monde as Two-Nostrils Cohen,
Sun Yat-Sen's breath checker. His victims call him at untoward hours.
His janitor bullies him, his wife cheats, he's the butt of his children's scorn,
and that's not all. (Slide, please.)

Yes, Excellency, we have a message from Isosceles Triangle.
Sebastopol activity is as always. Yevsky replaces the handpiece.
Count Trebishevsky's batman relates how the count
gets himself buried at sea for shits and giggles,
flag-draped wrap, captain mumbling appropriate words, whoosh and
    splash.
Nobody dies reading a poem. Furthermore,

poetry is often easy, witness this image of a winsome rusalka perched on a
    bough
overlooking a pond (slide, please). The poet, as much at sea as you,
propels himself in any direction by placing the palm of his hand
on his occiput and pushing. Poetry, especially on arrival,
cannot perform wonders at the snap of a finger.
Example: A case contains a violin.
Notwithstanding its pedigree (slide, please), skillful execution remains the
    issue,
especially if the floor collapses and a dazed survivor is willing to testify.
The face is skeletal, a spastic phantom in the guttering candle light.
Disturbed, it shifts to a vacant patch.
This is no time for a czardas.

Stemware tinkling, servers wafting by, silver trays as if afloat, a dash of
    laughter here,
taffeta rustle there, auburn hair's provocative whisper.
Has she a pouty, fleece-dusted mons or forbidding thatch patch?
I wonder what her socks smell like. I wonder as I wander.

Lapis lazuli eyes, faithful as marbles. He who has the gift of flight,
if he could navigate poetically, might say, Thanks, but no. Too risky.
Art is neither Life with its damps and panics nor Death with its moldy
    salamis.
The blind seek harmonic luminosities
with gestures and collisions. He lifts his only face
as if a beachball on a column of air, his hands modeling phantoms.
He tries to applaud, as a gesture perhaps of finality or futility,
and falls into unidentified cavities (slide, please).

In an especially bellicose fever-dream
the poet sees himself as a Z-scale General Sherman
marching to a sea about the size of a shuffle board.
War is hell.

A correspondent recently said he has never seen anyone succeed
in straightening a warped mind and does not think it possible. Not so!
I straightened a warped mind several years ago and so it remains.
I supported the rim at four points, convex side upward. I then placed
an unopened 46-ounce can of (from concentrate) tomato juice on the
        apex and let it sit
for two weeks. When I removed the can the mind was straight.
    Remember,
a ceremonial elephant is less than the sum of its weisswurst (slide, please).
    One
is the poorer for hearing the whimpers but rich in memories.

Seeking love or at the very least approval, one rakes a coy gaze from
prospect to prospect. Ah, Love, with your odd aftertastes,
whoever heard too much? We cannot from appearances seem to get
        enough.
He who is without Love is that dampness in the moonlight
come to a sorry pass. One's friends cry Yes! See him stride to the defense
        of
just about anything, and soon, walking along a spiral-shaped land,
one exhales dead air and smells really bad, but dear still to one's friends.
Read these lines in reverse in order to befuddle the sniper with picnic gas.
(Slide, please.)

PATHS TO THE CALIPH'S BOUDOIR

Some of us know too much about the caliph's path to the boudoir.

The reader looks frazzled as though somewhere about his, her or its
       person
the Frazzle Bonanza, behind which the beveled cottage
where Art degrades as follows:
One, inadequate lighting.
Two, inadequate bedrest.
Three, inadequate applicants.

Umbrella in hand, secured with a strip of old carpet, Lincoln practiced
       law
drifting from one courthouse to the next in his stovepipe hat.
A visitor looking down from the gallery said,
A coincidence, think you, that an ungrammatical cipher
should be using Lincoln's classiest words?
Ages before we consider the question Lincoln made his famous
Pronounce My Name Right speech. The second l is silent.
It resides in a shallow puddle.
The uppermost balcony cheered, Hoorah for Abe, he's heaving into vogue
any moment now! A few Septembers on, sharpshooters
tick corncobs off stalks. A nation mourns.

Add happiness to anonymity and you've giddy chaos.
Collect a mass of fleeting impressions
and if you're not careful, children show up.

Se la face ay pale keep it anyway. They're difficult to replace.
Eat fresh fruit. Avoid pet chops lest you suffer the anguish
of departure from the family circle. Remember,
nature begins as a small take-home zoo and patience.
And set aside time for collisions.

A man stubs his toe and despairs of ever walking it off. A child fries an
      onion.
Someone you have never seen ignores you
despite your best efforts to remain aloof. A butcher weeps,
matted sawdust at his feet. A policeman directs traffic invisible to the
      untrained eye
and likewise inaudible. A moving van slams into a dwelling
the occupants of which pop skyward.
The raptor misnamed cudgelwort sinks its talons into aspic,
a model of composure.

Tell the sheik I'm halvah from Basra but drop me somewhere else.

Success, beloved, like a bedtime skirmish, is a question of circumstance
over palette. Tell them how alluring I looked. As to laughter, spewed
      coleslaw,
porcelain caps (or amalgam), a loose tongue and

                America's story
                                      British fleet here
French fleet here
                      Poetry here

Adrift among shabby replicas, the poet's croutons are as unique
as New Year's Eve at the Soybean Foundation.
A supine position cushions transition.
Dogwoods burst into bloom specifically for rentiers.

Sometimes I hum in the bushes. One day I sat in a pail
and squat-waddled into town indifferent as a monarch in stucco. Keep
your pencils sharp as low-cost entertainment. The fool says,
I am equal to anything. The wise man says,
Even the cork tastes good when you see its little head
peeping at you over the tabletop. Mushrooms
are at their best when they stand evenly and don't talk back.
Does the pugilist look upon his punching bag as a hardy perennial? A city
    mouse,
it knows its bodegas. Don't drink from bedpans. A statue in the park
is worth ten in the head. The skeptic says, I doubt I made it. The cynic
    says,
Shove it anyway.

Two handy metaphors:
Budgeting on a shoestring. An anvil on a shoestring.

We abandon Young Werther to his expired sorrows.

My sister-in-law and her husband bought a place in a crater. To be on the
    safe side
they dug a storm cellar and set up a periscope. Mozart lies
in someone else's grave. It was only gas. The physician heard it,

the receptionist heard it, people in the waiting room heard it,
passersby and idlers heard it, the town, the world!
Set the table as low as you can and eat with your toes.

As for Syria, Abu creamed his only chicken. Some months later,
a few steps behind the wave of the future, tapirs sing ungulate blues,
best perhaps to close the window.

Poetry seeks opticians who measure for mind's-eye monocles.
My mandate and I, we wear the pants.
Aim nozzle at sky and squeeze. Stick your bimbo under the lid.
False dawn on an Ali Baba gurney, trussed and labeled In Spite of Oneself,
much as an uneasy vapor fumbles toward the preterit.

She bounced down some steps and murmured Uncle, or maybe it was
      Murphy.
I write a poem, nobody notices. I throw my left arm across the restaurant,
this they notice, the swine.

Zoltan, eat the fucking figs! Plink!
The poet departs like a blade through meringue.
O Poetry, thanks to you I'm as alive as an astonished lemur,
the poet of whom it has been said, See! He's real!
An assignment? A hobby? A passion? Dare you begrudge me my slot
in the Great Scheme of Things and wish on me the buboes?
That from which Faith hangs is, like an axe, the very picture of clarity,
so sleep with one eye open. Remaining with the ferrous, life is a large,
      cast-iron

get-well card. One's time is better spent combing coastal dunes for rose
    hips.
One's tongue fashions one's words' worth.
I'd love to talk longer but my tongue, King Author, is out for repairs.
Allah stuffs the stars with starlight. The clouds are sacks of wine
slung over the backs of camel mountains. I see in this crater, Uncle Feq,
little miracle ladies running around in small, miraculous circles.

Joseph Ignace Guillotin supposed the condemned, his neck as one with
    the fetters,
could wish himself a witness to the morning toilette of acacia trees
with their fragrant seepages. Climate is hard on snowmen.
Say you they're workmen loafing in slush? There is in nature
no moment more awesome than the mention of a taboo with its
    companion outburst
in the sacristy. Moslems en route to Mecca subsist on the contents of
    reliquaries
(just add water). They ponder the despondency of lost-wax figures (slide,
    please).

It requires the merest effort to see in this peanut
a woman unwilling to settle for anything less than oneself.

I once had a duck that laid a big pearl I gave to the czar.
There was joy in the Winter Palace.
And yet and too often, life's an empty igloo but for shed toes.
O beautiful literary park, he is here of whom it has been said he is
    elsewhere.

Now, natural as a road, whee! this movement! this crazy, vertiginous
 movement to, um,
Chingachgook, where are we? And there we see soldiers so admirably
 placed,
such martial beauty. The general sighs and spanks the monkey. Think of
 it!
A mighty fleet of prairie schooners, some as long as the red man's
 longhouse,
some as long as Calvinist sermons! There exists a bloom ice squelches to
 goo.
The Esquimaux, they slurp it, a mood intervenes, et voila!
re-entry with pride and little silver fishies, big, bulbous whales,
avuncular walrus, official seals, zigzaggy mollusks,
aquatic entertainment!

If ever you float away like a poached egg
on a whiff of indecision, bonhomie is unlikely but
perhaps a fortune awaits.

The Enchanted Kielbasa

An die ferne Geliebte

It begins just south of dragon scat, thence to the tongue,
images issued and hung out to drip,
(with walnuts).

ANVIL ON A SHOESTRING

Do stuffed somnambulists dream stuffed dreams?
When woolly forms l'azure obscure,
below, in Arles,
do Arlésiennes care? Beloved? You there?

Envoy:

Whether or not it's won her love
his poem's nectar degrades to sludge
& drips on a hapless lover's head.

THE ENCHANTED KIELBASA

Observe the suitor his shattered heart hauling
across ICUs in spent stents littered
as if a pet aortally tethered.

Poetry is the call of despondency's claxon.
Images such as this make a minefield of a mind
with you, Beloved, among the missing.

THE ENCHANTED KIELBASA

One infers bushes on unmet Beloveds
   as free-form proscenia.

ANVIL ON A SHOESTRING

Ere fortune sent me thee
I dined on anorexics
more in the way of paradox than need or conviction,
like drowning in a vat of restoratives. Intricate as a Norden
    bombsight,
delicate as a fishbone array,
behold the Beloved, with her cantilevered aura!

THE ENCHANTED KIELBASA

Lover shelters under tree.
Tree drops limb on lover.
Animistic gesture.

I dally in my fantasies at cunts that taste like lobster Cantonese.

THE ENCHANTED KIELBASA

Inform them of the merits of a microbe-rich diet
whilst I immerse myself in a top-quality sealant to last longer
for you, Beloved.

To offer condolences to the blade reducing oneself to muck on its task's conclusion is perverse. It is similarly perverse to propose a liaison with a disemboweled vapor.

THE ENCHANTED KIELBASA

Lover's lament, umlaut clouds.

ANVIL ON A SHOESTRING

When out of kinesis I run & a monument become
passersby will snap off remembrances
& I shall dwindle.
In his student days a pharmacist wallowed in a big unguent
(he was not alone). The old cropduster
flies now on memories as locusts alight and devour
their substance. You'd drop in & then you'd go
slamming the door so hard behind
a tooth departs its socket.

THE ENCHANTED KIELBASA

She reclines with, in her lap, a solemn figure in lignum vitae grasping its cock, from somewhere in Bali.

ANVIL ON A SHOESTRING

Here! For you! A romanza I play
on the organ from which nectar floweth,
a time to get up and a time to get downeth,
and O! I would, indeed O! I would,
were I other than at this fucking poemeth!

THE ENCHANTED KIELBASA

"Ah, such moans! I have no answer to squawks.
But I do enjoy the panting. You've a generous nature."
"As do you, my poet." She rows me away.
And so one departs, trousers over bowsprit.
It comforts to know snug harbors lie ahead
or that one runs aground in viscous verse.

Love mirrors love (motel ceilings),
with echo effects (fucking in cisterns)
& sometimes explosions (terrorists).
Call me shallow but mention as well
how these sighs in a chest dwell
filled with parts too large to swallow
& so must be one's Maker's doing.
(I threw that in.)

THE ENCHANTED KIELBASA

She falls out of bed & all about rumbles,
a buttocky sunset missing the chute.

A figurative scalpel excises memories
in a mind as well ordered as a Lego garden.

THE ENCHANTED KIELBASA

He sobs & she listens.
Sobbing still, he departs for the crater.
"Bowing from the waist, I'll pitch forward
And get stuck in a crack," he says & ducks.
"It will take but a moment & resembles a mystery."

The adorable paratroopess alights on Mister Happy.
Good things come to him who waits.

THE ENCHANTED KIELBASA

Muttonfat sunrise,
presage to a jaded day,
finds consonance with our premium cookware
stuck fast by means of a chef's goodwill & hardware.
O yes I'll love you though we die of white sauces,
as many even as keys at Steinway's,
plus Chiclets & dentures in repose.
You mean everything to me, Blanche.

Hers is a goddess's beauty
but she is skinny. Really, she is nothing
but a crack in the ceiling. Unknown to Cupid,
Psyche has crabs & I have piles
of poems.

THE ENCHANTED KIELBASA

You slid down the hill for me?
I see you've arrived with Pleistocene debris.
I also see a rock with a bronze plaque stating
that this is the spot where you stopped, Jacque-
line, & when,
tho it fails to say why.

ANVIL ON A SHOESTRING

Longings broadcast like wort spores.
I long to adjust you. I long to trim your opalescent fingernails
of unsightly cuticle, to excise turnips from your lissome silhouette
& your nacreous incisors from this model of composure, myself.
I see amidst spent cuticle-suppressors
one exquisitely honed fingernail for sending me packing,
my fat social ass a blip on the horizon.

THE ENCHANTED KIELBASA

I awoke in your arms,
I could not believe it,
my eyelids as with yardsticks bepropped.
I looked at the hole up there in the ceiling
over the spot where you said adieu.
I could not believe it,
my eyelids as with flagpoles bepropped.
I looked around me,
I could not believe it,
my eyelids as with pipelines bepropped.
As I say, I could not believe it.

I arrive, queen among women, through
granite & other of earth's densities chawed
by yr hmbl svnt. Excelsior therefore:
let cloud-gazers mark our cavortings.

THE ENCHANTED KIELBASA

A golden ray lighting our loving
would indeed be flattering, darling;
true, we are not deities,
yet nether are we these flashlit brutes
each beaming its birthright device
on a fellow brute's privacy, the overall effect,
however engaging,
bringing me back to you.

Wept to such a desiccant state, I need crafted a tear-oozing mask
I fuel by means of this wee rubber bladder secreted here
                              in my BVDs,
   the better used Balzac as regards you.

THE ENCHANTED KIELBASA

A woman came to me speaking womanese,
which I do not understand as fully as I ought
and was no little perplexed.
Moments later
angels descended linked like sausages,
speaking angel words;
I was, accordingly, perplexed exponentially.

That settles it.
I am yours & you are mine & just as soon as we quit swooning
over our good fortune we will cover each other
with little attentions.

THE ENCHANTED KIELBASA

"It wants better than antlers to outfit a lodge."
No sooner mentioned than furnishings appear,
with an upholstered chinrest at her crotch.

I would, the tentative, kiss her so
notwithstanding a hinged ear with spikes.

THE ENCHANTED KIELBASA

She is smaller than he remembers & colicky
& deaf. Sometimes, when he brings the hammer to his member
lying there athwart Love's anvil,
he has regrets.

ANVIL ON A SHOESTRING

The predators are so many neither can they amble nor loft
but lean, unsated, cheek to jowl to beak to needle proboscis.
Innocents swing on uglyfruit vines mere inches above gnashing jaws.
O! I want so to bathe this tableau in teardrops!
Are you ill? well-wishers ask. How to reply? Icecaps melt,
continents drift, and
one's manhood does its thing, cyclopean & poised.

THE ENCHANTED KIELBASA

The lovesick walrus nasalizes in slush.
To linger nasalizing in slush,
that's determination.
The Alute maiden sneezes on the trading post merry-go-round.
To sit on a painted walrus, sneezing, getting free rides,
that's lubrication.

ANVIL ON A SHOESTRING

A person, hospital birthed, of middling culture,
predictably discomfited dropped in a well,
who swallows his spit in conventional wise,
whose uppermost flaw:
just as you or I, Beloved, live mayhap on borrowed time,
he goes abroad in borrowed pants,
& the other, the lender, too shy to call out,
subsists on reflux & (ach!) the years . . .

THE ENCHANTED KIELBASA

The Silesian cow tree is indeed milkable
but those who therefrom suckle fall ill
& no few perish. Ruttish boys know the thing in the fissure
tho it like as not clamp down for good (or not so good),
moments best forgot. She showers me daily with a nose cannonade
she calls postnuptial rice. And so to dreams: Cleopatra!
A delicate business—the Queen of the Nile is dead.
A rasp across the waking heart!

So utterly provocative, the Beloved is herself without sleep.
Is't our wed pulses the love nest undoing or universality tic-resonant?
Be she hourglass or sand-stuffed immortal
upside down and over again, or over again or over?
If in fact and over again, one musicks one's member
with bugled Retreat through mouthpieceless lips,
cascading thence to the kitchenette
to assist the kielbasa with its anguished memoir, *Had I Urethra*
or, worse, had you mine. If the latter, likewise (again).

THE ENCHANTED KIELBASA

One's Beloved wanders off at six mph,
oneself, next, at four,
meeting never, seeking ever, weeping & combing th'orb.

A miracle! crieth he, pointing to a tree
at a felon or red squirrel or (praise be!) one's Beloved.

The midday clock at a particulate-dense distance
recalls the semaphore, Palmer Method.

The sphinx that loved me expired. Its urogenital system
droops over the tablecloth (an Oedipal touch). As to the jaws,
the speaker has only to keep the hinges in good working order
as a charm to the speaking voice. Nasality (a fault)
takes talk for a walk through the nose's clothes whereas
postnasality closes the nose to olfaction
as the organism rises in poem-assisted transubstantiation
to a better place.

THE ENCHANTED KIELBASA

A memory of what we shared:
a teddy bear which, when squeezed, declares
Accept no fucking substitutes!

From the Universal Pervasive, opportunity seized. Attend:
You are imagined, whom I upend to nibble,
sniff & envision,
lest clairvoyants eavesdrop, permissiver environs,
which is to say, less.

Reduced, like ruins, to significant bulges,
you become, au fond, an upturned goatee,
a gentle, absorbing smile.

THE ENCHANTED KIELBASA

The dwarf stuck fast in a knothole
pretending he's Nothung, or better, Sumthung:
He looks to his heart at a little blue devil
ankle deep in imposture.

ANVIL ON A SHOESTRING

Chance in season coconuts drops & lust in season tumesces the
    smitten.
Lust seduces immortals even! whose cloud-pillowed humpings
by moonlight mirror in the puddled ruts I negotiate
to be here with you. There's no need to speak.
Rather savor these conceits, all of which you could store in a pore.

THE ENCHANTED KIELBASA

The love-hungry submariners torpedo girls at the beach with wursts
and She, the Beloved, dozing off at the Bösendorfer,
pitches forward, the appurtenances of her cherished physiognomy
striking a chord the significance of which alludes all analysis,
as do these madmen the Coast Guard's best efforts.

The Beloved: a cafeteria in which
misunderstanding floats on yesterday's soup.
Her amorous glances: a dusk in which
everybody decides to get out of the house
and collide. But I am being vague.

THE ENCHANTED KIELBASA

The night I fled the metropolis I tripped over a sofa
on which, Beloved, you lay, anointing yourself with scents.

Life in the country:
I am reminded, Beloved, to tell you that your eyelid quivers
when you whisper in my ear and that the cow seems embarrassed,
averts her head and stops chewing.

Duodenal Etiquette
Scènes de Ballet

PUNCH, WITH PADDLE
JUDY, WITHOUT PADDLE

PUNCH:

Perfection? Pfui! Return it to peerless source!
She cooks, gavottes, blue spark as clean as, in liquidity awash,
but nay I say, she will not do.
Bring on the lady's twin, Aurora Sunset Midday Yin
(no kin to yen, currency or urge), followed by Ying,
& better than either or even forever, & so on, etcetera,
at last enmeshed where Quotidia tugs
tasseled gliss&i & frolicsome bugs. (Whack!)
I dashed off in haste: Mere moments away from ominous pings,
accountancy's fugues, essence of otter,
Destiny's tutus encircling daughters,
palpability's badinage,
a fusillade by spasms arrayed,
alighting lightly on the splayed,
a setting for a gropes, by which crass device the race lopes along
as deconstructs the deck callèd poop. I hear you, Hosanna,

a Mae West requesting out there in the saline goop,
your spinto urgencies surplusly befouling
aqueous frills in the deep's embrace.
One squints to intuit tomorrow's erasures,
comes away with an ardent Inuit,
excellent benefits, perks. (Whack!)

JUDY:

Ere we befouled our bespoke jodhpurs
merest motes in th'aether were, disfiguring matter
with imprecise skills.

Read into gestures ends before spleens,
dirigible dreams,
dank motets in bile braised,
sutured harmonics, anchors aweighed.

Can bunting mask an assassin's world-view?
Camouflage farts?
Provide the glue for klunky mesostics?
Flat-out erotics?
A Phillips-head screw? (O surly yew!)
Be Hugo Boss's Siegfried line?
A varietal whine? A rheum with ague?

I dashed off in haste: He wears a giant sheetrocker's scowl!
I dashed off in haste: He brandishes a two-ton trowel!
I dashed off in haste: At anti-matter he fusses & fumbles,
stately as portals to outst&ing venues,
bigger even than tectonic bungles!

Stuffing feathers up his nose!
Inhaling! Inhaling! Feathers no more!

Punch:

J'adore your leg. (Whack!)
I note the point at which your leg tolerates anything,
an observation I file under Marvels Relating to Limbs.
Other possibilities?
Ramen Lao Da's Ramen Da Xiao,
Jie's Ramen One Thing / Two,
Crayfish Ramen,
Raimondo's stew bleu.

After the rain, gazing at the glistening treetops,
his sister mutters dreamily, "Aspen, aspirin,
aspersions cast & casting . . ."
He, likewise dreamily, lays his neck athwart a stump
awaiting a hooded passerby,
th'aspens whisp'ring, "Breeze . . ."

I clap clamshells in hope of becoming a percussionist.
I require tutelage.

Two potatoes, three. The aspins' sighs,
this must wait or seem to, pig, & thinking so, see . . . (Whack!)

Judy:

Women almost hear them, swains in pits hastily dug.
Marmots mayhap?

At length we encounter a sky-like expanse
a touch too lacy, too long pants,
a too big hat under which one recalls
st&ing atop a discomfited child, its urgent "Uhn!"
suggesting what? Disaffection?
When I am old enough to ask, you will be dead.

Brighter stars were burning then, in 1692.
Among slate rooftops she abode, up spires shimmying,
herself, I mean, in olden times,
calling softly to yet softer clouds,
"Mousie dear? Are you there?"

Punch:

We anticipate what we loathe
or simmer. "Of what bonanza thinkest thou ill,
small smelly churl?" (Whack!)

The targets outnumber the marksmen. (Whack!)

This he is who, toothsome female? He who scuttles butts? (Whack!)
Is this the he of Cloudlet Eight where dreams are gratis, almost?
Who rang?

'Tis Low-Slung Hermal, pusher to the demi-monde. (Whack!)
"Drink & plough whomever you please. Ignore the cost
or may the devil do a hundred chin-ups,
taking moaning me in stride. It is many hours to infamy
& not quite time for din-din, my friend."
His mouth is much diminished.

He is otherwise our h&somest survivor.

Sump pumps pump however shallow the sentiment.

Judy:

Out here in Nature I'm really really happy
in teensy tiny ways, wooo hooo!
Froggies in my panties!

Nothing makes me happier than peaceful buttered noodles,
the merest hint of companionship,
& thinking about—who else?—myself,
A Levantine doxy formerly, now a big, fat thought. I mean forever,
strangler.
Desire compounds the difference
especially on a pedestal. Can you hear me now?
How all my plans turn to l&fill? Be that as it may,
Project 31 ("Flemish Lint") is rolling right along,
donations are pouring in, lots of fabric, & I will sew until
my beating heart's humanitarian core is as content
as a chrysanthemum.

Punch:

& then? (I really meant "when?") (Whack!)
Flurry, blizzard, slush
& Dowl&, dead.
"Can we excuse our wrongs . . .?"

The Legend of Chief Sequoia (He Makes Her Squeak)
Printemps!—renewed longings for that of which
one never gets enough, & above all else,
working well with others. (Whack!)

I am attractive, tell me your address,
I'll send you a merkin on & off.
Tell me your address, I'll send myself
at the end of the trail, trial, travails . . . a problem withal for
social engineering.
If you'd like to attend, please just be & leave it to me.
We'll remark how we differ.
In short, improvisation. (Whack!) Or perhaps
improvement.

The Dada Within

E ARE FORTUNATE as a society that certain endeavors require certification. Should I one day awaken convinced I've an aptitude for reconstructive oral surgery, pediatric oncology, gastroenterology, ophthalmology, veterinary medicine or, sidewise, electrical engineering, it would not be unreasonable to haul me away in a strait jacket. At the very least you'd best decline my offer to rewire your home. Or neuter your kitten.

However, "It's a free country" obtains in practices less available to prosecutorial scrutiny. Charlatans come fast to mind, especially in the God dodge. To explore deeper here would plunge me into a simmering rage, nor do I propose to impose on the reader's patience.

Obviously, given our context, we're about the arts. Creativity. Dare we say it, sublimity. The transcendental. From certain angles and in a certain light, the divine. The Good Lord willin' and the crapper don't back up, when all goes flawlessly, unreasonably—nay, miraculously—well, something interesting might happen. While it's true that art schools and writing workshops exist, with proofs of attendance moreover, individuals can with a clear conscience declare themselves artists or writers, or maybe both in the same carcass, on the strength of a say-so.

"I'm a writer."

"Have you published anything?"

"Not yet."

Therefore and so forth and by my green candle, to state one's theme, I am in the great tradition of soi-disantitude a full-feathered Dada innocent of validation beyond the skin I occupy. Nihil obstat. Devil take the hindmost. Damn the torpedoes but be mindful of the reef.

To which forebears is one especially beholden? To Marcel Duchamp, certainly. His lifelong insouciance remains a standard to emulate, not to neglect the ready-made, Art's tectonic shift. In a broader sense, to Alfred Jarry and his assault on propriety. I stand in particular admiration of his gift to humankind, 'pataphysics, an as yet immeasurable leap beyond metaphysics. Yet am I reluctant to acquire membership in the Collège de Same Name inasmuch as this requires application and (I'm guessing) a registration fee. From a respectful distance I continue to admire 'pataphysics' embrace of imaginary solutions, no less the impertinent apostrophe. Assigning to the already large Cosmos an exponential expansion, more likely infinite, introduces freedoms as gratifying as good afternoon sex.

THE DADA WITHIN

We won't complicate the discussion with Thespis's offspring. Further, I'll endeavor to keep autobiography to a barely audible mumble, notwithstanding some good stuff, e.g., my having deflowered Shirley Temple. For another time. *The Dada Within* is a topic—to be hoped—of general interest and application. Indeed, but what do you mean by Dada, granddad?

Can we agree to call it a free-wheeling, sometime destabilizing state of mind?

To begin, my identification with Dada flounders in anachronism. Call it twilit senescence. Geriatric willfulness. I align with the originals in the Cabaret Voltaire despite having little in common, least of all one's wardrobe. Europe, at the height of a rather fastidious civilization, descended into a war the duration and ferocity of which took all by surprise. The machine gun played a prominent role. (I digress: given the run on guns and the price of ammunition, when available—blame the pandemic and the right wing's tribal drift—shooting a fully automatic weapon at a range is a luxury just south of Patek Philippe. I ought to have mentioned earlier that one's Jarry admiration also looks to sidearms. The reader may know of this anecdote. Jarry was shooting his revolver in a backyard. A neighbor complained that this reckless behavior endangered her son. Should that possibility become a reality, Jarry offered to help the lady make another.)

Anger, disillusion, cynicism, la vie bohème's persistent undertow, all (as the narrative has it) explain why Dada popped up at its moment in history. At a far remove from the War to End All Wars it pleases this fantasist to think that absurdity's cultivation and matution better describe Dada's precious bodily fluids as and where they nowadays flow.

Does a sharply drawn line between Dada and Surrealism exist? Hardly. Or maybe. Or no. Or yes. A good deal of Surrealist art seems to me Dada in spirit. Max Ernst's painting of the Virgin Mother spanking a young Jesus's bare ass, with Surrealism's heavy hitters looking on through a window is pure Dada. Freud's subconscious plays no role in this psychodrama. René Magritte's work is Surrealist in its dream-like aspect and Dada in its drollery. This can be said: Surrealism in its French heyday was authoritarian. Andy Breton ran a tight ship. More than a few heretics walked the plank. The Dadas were anarchic. A favorite Dada object, Man Ray's *Gift*, is an upright clothing iron, its plate lined down the center with a row of spikes (glued nails, actually). It was my great good luck to find a miniature wooden ironing board of the same period, intended, I believe, for shirt sleeves, to which, in homage, I glued a line of nails and hung on a wall—a footnote to a brilliant absurdity.

As a writer, I identify with participants in a movement I might well have regarded with suspicion and, who knows, disdain were I a contemporary in fact rather than tepid spirit. As a good, law-abiding bourgeois, this anachronistic impulse began a ton of years ago and continues with chance operations—the gathering of printed motleys I fashion into images, thoughts and associations that, when all goes well, engage and perhaps even startle and amuse. I welcome beauty to remain in the beholder's eye. Nor am I much concerned with the participation of my subconscious or unconscious. They're on their own. Look, if the superficial dazzles, depth need not apply. Think of spectral insects skimming across a still pond, lightly disturbing the water's surface. In bright sunlight. With frogs. Lily pads even.

Mike Silverton's poetry appeared in the late '60s and '70s in numerous periodicals and anthologies. He produced poetry readings for The New School for Social Research, New York's municipal radio station, WNYC, and Pacifica Radio's WBAI, KPFA, and KPFK. One glaring regret: Mike had arranged to record Frank O'Hara on the week in which he was killed, fateful weekend intervening, by a dune buggy.

Mike's music writing, centering on modernist classical, has appeared in *Fanfare*, his own *LaFolia.com*, and elsewhere. He has also reviewed high-end audio hardware for *Fanfare*, *The Abso!ute Sound* and *The StereoTimes.com*.

In early 2002, he and his wife Lee relocated to an 1842 house and barn in Midcoast Maine, where he indulged an interest in assemblage of an etiolated Dada persuasion, resulting in several works in a group show at The Center for Maine Contemporary Art in Rockport, and a one-man show at Belfast's Aarhus Gallery.

www.ingramcontent.com/pod-product-compliance
Lightning Source LLC
Chambersburg PA
CBHW020200090426
42734CB00008B/882